NEW YORK

Eve

D0351465

New York is a vibrant, over-the-top cosmopolitan city with unflagging energy and a competitive streak whether on Wall Street or in the arts. It grew up vertically on a handful of islands watched over by the Statue of Liberty, amid noise and frenzied activity, ever intent on doing things bigger and faster. Today, the city has re-emerged even stronger after the deadly attacks of 9/11. Manhattan stretches from the East River to the Hudson, a checkerboard of narrow glass canyons and shady streets of townhouses. It has many faces: sophisticated along Fifth Avenue, bohemian and intellectual in Greenwich Village, bustling on Times Square and Broadway, bucolic in Central Park, artistic in Chelsea, trendsetting in TriBeCa, Soho and NoLIta. Visitors have an infinite choice of things to do: museums, music, art galleries, theater – Broadway and off. The borough of Brooklyn, Manhattan's sprawling neighbor, is no less fascinating, with its diverse lively 'villages' (Dumbo, Williamsburg, Cobble Hill), a mix of elegant brownstones, lofts and warehouses taken over by artists and writers. Further on, the melting pot of Queens is home to Greeks, Chinese, Hispanics and many more. The city is dotted with neighborhood cafés, lounge bars, diners, restaurants serving food from all over the globe, flea markets, boutiques, jazz clubs, arts venues... All these, and more, are now within your reach, thanks to this MapGuide.

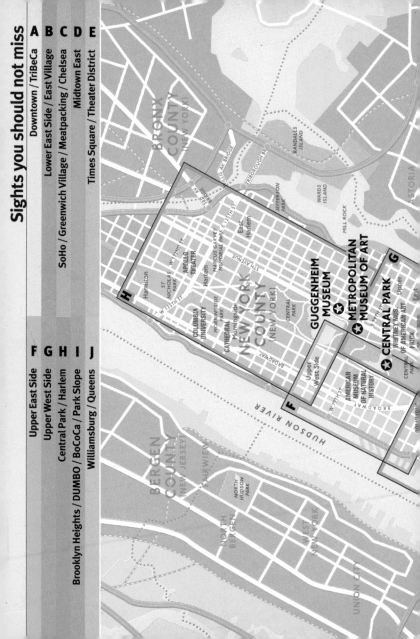